परिवार
Parivaar
family
The art of living life

R.N. Kogata • Lalita Kogata

AF518663

D.K. Printworld (P) Ltd.
New Delhi

Cataloging in Publication Data — DK
[Courtesy: D.K. Agencies (P) Ltd. <docinfo@dkagencies.com>]

Kogata, R. N. (Ram Narayan), 1964–
Parivaar = Family : the art of living life/R.N. Kogata, Lalita Kogata.
p. cm.
English and Hindi.
ISBN 13: 9788124605769
ISBN 10: 8124605769

1. Families — Prayers and devotions. 2. Families in art. 3. Siva (Hindu deity) — Art. 4. Parvati (Hindu deity) — Art. 5. Gaṇeśa (Hindu deity) — Art. 6. Hindu art. I. Kogata, Lalita, 1965-, joint author. II. Title. III. Title: Family : the art of living life.

DDC 704.9426 22

First Published in India, 2011
ISBN 13: 978-81-246-0576-9
ISBN 10: 81-246-0576-9

A Creation of:
Mr. R.N. Kogata
Mrs. Lalita Kogata
608, Hiran Magari, Sector-11, Udaipur - India
Phone : +91-94141-58870, +91-294-2583870
devkush@rediffmail.com

Published and printed by:
D.K. Printworld (P) Ltd.
'Sri Kunj' F-52, Bali Nagar
Ramesh Nagar Metro Stn., New Delhi - 110 015
Phs.: 011-2545 3975, 2546 6019
Fax: 011-2546 5926
Email: indology@dkprintworld.com
Web: www.dkprintworld.com

परिवार
Parivaar
family
The art of living life

माता च पार्वति देवी, पिता देवो महेश्वर ।
बान्धवा शिवभक्ता च, स्वदेशो भुवन त्रयम ॥

mātā ca pārvatī devī, pitā devo maheśvara ।
bāndhavā śivabhaktā ca, svadeśo bhuvana trayam ॥
— Śaṅkara's *Annapūrṇāṣṭakam*

(Pārvatī is my mother, Śiva (Maheśvara) is my father, all Śivabhaktas are my relatives (or family members) and all the three worlds are my abode.

पार्वती मेरी माता हैं, शिव (महेश्वर) मेरे पिता हैं, सारे शिव-भक्त मेरे सगे-सम्बन्धी हैं और तीनों लोक मेरे घर हैं।

॥ ॐ गं गणपतये नमः ॥

Preface

It is said that perhaps the greatest social service that can be rendered by anybody to his country and to the mankind is to bring up a good family. Remember, other things may change us, but we start and end with the family and the happiest moments of life would be the few which we all pass at home in the bosom of our family.

The family is the cornerstone of our society. More than any other force it shapes the attitude, the hopes, the ambitions, and the values of the child. And when the family collapses it is the children that are usually damaged. When it happens on a massive scale the community itself is crippled. So, unless we work to strengthen the family, to create conditions under which most parents and children will stay together, all the rest - schools, playgrounds, public assistance, and private concern will never be enough.

In a family, we talk together, we walk together, we laugh together, we cry together, love is shown, suffering is shared and the love for each other is never impaired.

We have plenty of examples even in our mythology when breakage or separation of family for any reason has made the family unhappy or even destroyed the whole family. We know about King Dasharatha, father of Lord Rama, whose family had suffered badly after the action of Kaikaiyee, wife of King Dasharatha. Rama and Laxmana along with Maa Sita had to leave for dwelling in the forest; King Dasharatha died remembering Lord Rama; Bharata, brother of Lord Rama never accepted to become the king in the absence of Lord Rama. Moreover, the family never returned in its original shape even after the return of Lord Rama from the forest. Ravana had to face the consequences after his brother Vibheeshana left his Kingdom, Lanka, and ultimately lost the battle to Lord Rama and even lost his life. Kauravas and Pandavas were never happy and peaceful after separation due to the ambitions of Duryodhana, the eldest amongst Kauravas and it even resulted in the death of all Kauravas and five sons of Pandavas, besides many others.

Each family has moments, moments of happiness and emotion. Moments that show love and kindness. Family is everything — family is always going to be there for you, family is the people you trust, family is the kind of people who care a lot about you, family is the first people you come to if you have a problem, just remember that family is going to be there, no matter what, in tough times, in everything.

No matter what you've done for yourself or for humanity, if you can't look back on having given love and attention to your own family, what have you really accomplished?

Inspired by these basics of a family, this book is a small try by us to express our thoughts and importance of having a family with the usual expectation of blessings from all of you.

We prostrate before our parents, Shri Bhairav Lal and Smt Kanchan Devi Kogata, and Prof. K. M. Nuwal and Smt Kamla Devi Nuwal, for their beloved blessings for reaching this stage.

R.N. Kogata
Lalita Kogata

Importance of Family

"Vasudhaiva Kutumbakam" — "the world is my family." Indian culture teaches us this motto, i.e. to treat all beings, animate and inanimate, in the world as our family members. In other words, we have to show our love and affection towards everything living and non-living and treat them with respect.

A Supreme Being or God runs the whole world. In it there are human beings like us, animals and birds, insects and worms, trees and plants, creepers and grass, mountains and stones, rivers and streams, etc. These constitute a very big family.

Our small family is run by a father and a mother. The father works and earns money, and with it the mother runs the household. Both look after the children in the best way possible.

God is all-Powerful and so he runs the world-family alone. Our parents always wish well and sacrifice their comforts to see that we children come up in life as intelligent, good and successful human beings. With enormous love and affection they ensure that we go on the right path, even by being strict and harsh sometimes. From where does this caring attitude flow? — the origin is God. God only comes in the form of father and mother to show his love towards his children — or in the form of Shiv and Parvati, Vishnu and Lakshmi, or Rama and Sita.

In the Hindu pantheon there is a famous family — that of Lord Shiv comprising his consort Parvati and children Ganesh and Kartika. They can be called the first family. As a mark of tolerance among the members of this family we can take the *vahanas* or vehicles normally associated with them. Shiv wears garlands of snakes which the peacocks eat — peacock is the vehicle of Kartika. Peacocks and snakes are the enemies of mouse or rat, the vehicle of Ganesh. Shiv's vehicle bull is a prey to lion, the vehicle of Parvati or Devi. If you look at the composite picture of this family with the vehicles, you will wonder how the animals, birds and reptile coexist amicably without any animosity.

We should take Lord Shiv's family as an ideal example and show our love and affection to all living beings. By adjusting themselves to any changed circumstances, and by destroying ego from their minds all members can stay together in a joint family.

People learn the traditions, culture and way of life from within a family. In India it is not uncommon to see four or five generations — related patrilineally — living together under one roof, eating together, working and cooperating in the family business or independent occupations. Women by convention or perforce go to live with their respective husbands in the big family household.

In spite of the impact of Western education and globalisation, the traditional joint family remains the ideal among Indians. One of the reasons for the success of the business communities in India is said to be the joint family system. In it the wealth is pooled together and made available to both skilled and unskilled members to start business. We can quote Dalmias, Tatas and Birlas from north India, and Chettiars and Mudaliars from the south as examples.

The trend now is towards nuclear families as opposed to joint families. A man, after marriage, lives with his wife and children independently within the same city or in another, depending upon his job compulsions. Where the wives also go to work, we can see, due to problem with job transfers, children's education, etc., even husbands and wives living separately in different locations, leaving the children in the care of the grandparents. Though living in nuclear families, all the members, bound by family ties, make it a point to join together at the time of a marriage or some important religious function in the main household.

Even where joint family system is not followed, for example, among poor agricultural workers and rural labour, the relatives live near each other so that the bond of kinship is maintained. This also helps in giving and taking financial and other help in times of need. This "living together" is more visible among the workforce from the villages living in big towns and cities and among the slum-dwellers. Here people from a particular region or state live together in clusters, which enable them to render help within the community and to demand from the authorities basic amenities as a group. These poor and illiterate people living in slums, constituting a sizeable portion of the population, are patronised by the political parties for their votes during elections.

Financial and social security plays an important part in groups living together and in joint families where even handicapped, unskilled and unemployed youths are also taken care of.

As joint families grow bigger, they divide ultimately into smaller units. This break-up is an inevitable response to several conditions like expansion of the family business, movement of members to other locations within the country or abroad, not unusually quarrels among members, family intrigues, property disputes, etc.

A family togetherness depends upon the role each member plays, and the members' sacrifices, devotion to ideals and respect to family values form the ladder to success.

परिवार हर्ष है, खुशी है, प्रसन्नता है।
परिवार के साथ से ही मकान घर बनता है।।

परिवार Parivaar family

Family is joy, is happiness, is pleasure.
Family's togetherness makes the house as home.

परिवार आधार है, मज़बूती है, विश्वास है।
परिवार के सदस्यों के मिलने का मौका हमेशा ख़ास है।।

Parivaar परिवार family

Family is base, is strength, is faith.
Family members' meeting together is always a special occasion.

परिवार अर्पण है, दर्पण है, समर्पण है।
परिवार खुशियों का संगम क्षण-प्रतिक्षण है।।

परिवार Parivaar family

Family is dedication, is mirror, is devotion.
Family has confluence of happiness every moment.

परिवार प्यार है, मोहब्बत है, अपनत्व है।
परिवार ज़िंदगी की सच्चाई का घनत्व है।।

परिवार Parivaar family

Family is love, is affection, is relation.
Family is density of the truth of life.

परिवार त्याग है, तपस्या है, सेवा है।
परिवार का साथ चलना भगवान का मेवा है।।

Parivaar परिवार family

Family is sacrifice, is penance, is service.
Family remaining together is the gift of God.

परिवार खुशियों का गुणा, दुखों का भाग है।
परिवार में प्रेम नहीं तो, खुशियाँ भी ख़ाक हैं।।

परिवार Parivaar family

Family is multiplication of happiness, division of sorrow.
Family without love converts the happiness also into ashes.

परिवार लड़ियां है, मोती है, माला है।
परिवार में हर व्यक्ति एक दूसरे का रखवाला है।।

परिवार Parivaar family

Family is string of pearl, is pearl, is garland.
Family's every person is protector of each other.

परिवार साथ है, हिम्मत है, हौंसला है।
परिवार चहचहाते पक्षियों का सुरक्षित घोंसला है।।

Family is company, is courage, is intrepidity.
Family is the safe snug of melodious singing birds.

परिवार पवित्रता है, भक्ति है, पूजा का शंख है।
परिवार आसमान में उड़ते हुए पक्षियों के पंख हैं।।

परिवार
Parivaar
family

Family is purity, is veneration, is conch of worship.
Family is feather of happily flying bird in the sky.

परिवार सुरक्षा है, सहभागिता है, शक्ति है।
परिवार चुप रहकर भी प्यार की अभिव्यक्ति है।।

Family is safety, is participation, is power.
Family is expression of love even with silence.

परिवार आवश्यकता है, ज़रूरत है, समाधान है।
परिवार में एक की सफलता भी सभी का सम्मान है।।

परिवार Parivaar family

Family is necessity, is need, is solution.
Family gets honour even by success of any one.

परिवार सरलता है, आज़ादी है, स्वतन्त्रता है।
परिवार हर व्यक्ति को चिन्तामुक्त रखता है।।

Parivaar परिवार family

Family is simplicity, is independence, is freedom.
Family keeps every one free from tension.

परिवार पढ़ाई है, ज्ञान है, परीक्षा है।
परिवार जीने की कला और संयम की शिक्षा है।।

Family is study, is knowledge, is exam.
Family is art of living and education of forbearance.

परिवार पर्वत है, आकाश है, ऊँचाई है।
परिवार सुखी जीवन की असली सच्चाई है।।

Family is mountain, is sky, is height.
Family is the real truth of happy life.

परिवार उजाला है, उज्जवलता है, रंगीनियाँ है।
परिवार अपने आप में सुखी और सम्पूर्ण दुनिया है।।

परिवार Parivaar family

Family is light, is brightness, is colourfulness.
Family in itself is happy und whole life.

परिवार आस्था है, नींव है, सन्तुलन है।
परिवार के बिन जीवन विस्तार नहीं, संकुचन है।।

परिवार Parivaar family

Family is reverence, is root, is balance.
Family's absence is not life's expansion but meanness.

परिवार को साथ रखने में आपका भी योगदान है।
परिवार में सभी का त्याग और समर्पण सफलता का सोपान है।।

परिवार Parivaar family

Family's togetherness has important role from you also.
Family members' sacrifice and devotion is the ladder of success.

परिवार में सब सुखी रहें, यही मेरा सपना है।
परिवार में सबका साथ रहे, भगवान से यही प्रार्थना है।।

परिवार Parivaar family

Family members all live happily, this is my dream.
Family of everyone lives together, It is my prayer to God.